THE DAY OF THE COWBOY

KENNETH ULYATT

I'm a rowdy cowboy, just off the stormy plains,
My trade is cinchin' saddles and pullin' bridle reins,
O I can tip the lasso, boys, it is with graceful ease,
I can rope a streak of lightnin' and ride it where I please.

I'm Bound to Follow the Longhorn Cows

LONGMAN YOUNG BOOKS   *Explorer 8*

Acknowledgements

The publishers and author would like to thank the following for their kind permission to reproduce the photographs, paintings and drawings appearing in this book :

Amon Carter Museum, Fort Worth, Texas : pp. 8 and 9, 28, 33, 37, 42 ; The Bancroft Library : p. 11 ; S. D. Butcher Collection, Nebraska State Historical Society : p. 46 ; California Historical Society : p. 21 ; Denver Public Library, Western History Department : p. 17 ; Erwin E. Smith Collection of Pictures of Range Life, Library of Congress : pp. 24–5, 38 and 39, 40, 41, 48 ; Library of Congress : pp. 5, 13 ; The Mansell Collection ; pp. 6, 7 ; Montana Historical Society : p. 1 ; Northern Natural Gas Company Collection, Joslyn Art Museum, Omaha, Nebraska : p. 8 ; Ruth Koerner Oliver : cover, pp. 16, 44 and 45 ; Stanford University Archives : p. 30 ; Union Pacific Railroad : p. 31 ; Western Reserve Historical Society : p. 18 ; Winchester Press, N.Y. : p. 34, 35.

The songs on the title page and back cover are taken from Lomax, The Folk Songs of North America, *Cassell & Co, 1960.*

LONGMAN YOUNG BOOKS
A Division of Penguin Books Ltd,
Bath Road, Harmondsworth, Middlesex

Text Copyright © 1973 by Kenneth Ulyatt
Diagrams and maps copyright © Penguin Education 1973

First published 1973

ISBN 0 582 15385 9

Printed in Great Britain by
W. S. Cowell Ltd at the Butter Market, Ipswich

WIDE-EYED, the cattle looked over the side as the blue waters slid by. They were sharp-horned, nimble animals and they had to be quick-footed to keep upright on the deck of the little sailing ship as she altered course to get out of the path of a Spanish galleon, heading east.

It was 1521, just two years after Cortez had conquered all of Mexico with a tiny army of five hundred men and sixteen horses. The small herd of cattle belonged to a man called Gregorio de Villalobos. He had put them aboard the caravel at Santo Domingo, on the island of Hispaniola in the Spanish West Indies, and he was taking them to Mexico.

As he watched the towering galleon sailing by perhaps he wondered about the amount of Aztec treasure that she was taking back to Spain.

Perhaps the cattle bawled when they slipped on the spray-spewn decks and the ropes chaffed their necks.

Nobody records if they were seasick! Nobody even knows how many there were. Exactly where the caravel put into shore on that vast, newly-discovered continent, or where scrambling hoofs made the first cattle trail across the Mexican sand is not known either.

But although Villalobos may have had little thought beyond that of establishing a ranch to supply food for Cortez's conquering army, he was bringing to the New World a prize which, in the end, would prove far richer than all the gold of the Spanish conquests lumped together. He was bringing America the longhorn cows!

The Spaniards had two aims in the New World: they wanted to find gold, silver and precious stones, the wealth by which all power was measured. And they wanted to convert the people of the countries they conquered to Christianity.

In Mexico they found gold in abundance. And as treasure ship after treasure ship sailed back to Spain laden with the plunder of the Aztec Empire, the merchants who owned the ships began to see New Spain, as it was called, not only as a source of mineral wealth but as a market for their own products.

The native peoples of Mexico were soon put to work for their new masters. Great estates, or *estancias*, were established with the retired *conquistadors* living like little kings, ruling hundreds of slaves and importing goods from Europe.

And raising Spanish cattle!

For there were no cows on the new continent. Travellers to the north brought back vague rumours of a shaggy beast with massive shoulders, curved horns and small, dainty feet. But no cattle or horses; and so very quickly the venture of Villalobos began to bear fruit.

Ranchos spread inland from the coast, stocked with herds shipped from the Caribbean island colonies where the Spaniards had already built up a thriving industry with cattle from Spain. Emigrants followed the herds, bringing with them the expert knowledge of centuries. Soon, all Mexico was colonized. The

4

With a priest to guide them, sweating under heavy armour, some members of the party walking to give their horses a rest, the Spaniards cross the Great Plains in search of the Seven Cities of Gold. Painted by Frederic Remington, a famous Western artist.

Spanish way of life — Spanish houses, Spanish law, Spanish industry, Spanish language and Spanish religion — was being stamped rapidly and indelibly on the New World.

But all the time, the hunt for new empires of gold went on. For after Cortez's incredibly rewarding conquest of Mexico, and especially after another Spanish general, Pizarro, had stumbled across an equally rich civilization in Peru, the Spaniards could not believe that a third golden empire did not exist somewhere to the north.

To begin their new conquest they chose a point of land, a short distance from the Caribbean islands, which had been discovered at Easter in 1513 and named after the Easter festival of flowers, *Pascua Florida*. Three brave attempts were made to explore the hinterland. All failed through sickness and the hostility of the Indians.

Then, in 1528, Panfilo de Narvaez landed 600 men, with livestock and horses, on the west coast of Florida. He sent his ships

We call them conquistadors. To the Spaniards, they were adelantados, *the men who 'advanced' the boundaries of the Spanish Empire. This is a drawing of one of them by Remington. He has shown one of Coronado's soldiers, lance in hand, musket across his saddle, riding north towards the great plains. At his side is a foal from the herd of horses which accompanied the expedition. Coronado's soldiers were the first white men to see the Grand Canyon of Colorado.*

across the Gulf of Mexico to an agreed rendezvous while the land party endeavoured to march round the coast. The two parties never met. Harassed by Indians, scourged by disease, and very near starvation, the land column managed to reach Galveston Island. There, some eighty survivors split up. Some vanished into the wilderness; others, including the treasurer and second-in-command of the expedition, Nunez Cabeza de Vaca, were captured by Indians.

Five unbearable years later, near present-day San Antonio, de Vaca and two companions managed to escape and head west. Sometimes alone, sometimes with roving bands of friendly Indians, these white men wandered across a wonderful pastureland until, one day, they forded a great river and stumbled into the arms of a party of their fellow countrymen. They had reached Mexico!

What a tale these *hidalgos* had to tell. They had met many Indian tribes, shared their lives and learned their customs. They had crossed a lush country, the triangle of land formed by the junction of the Rio Grande and the Gulf coast . . . 'ideal cattle country', said de Vaca. The climate was warm, the grass green all the year round, the water plentiful from the tributaries of the rivers flowing south.

But this was not what their rescuers wanted to hear. They preferred the tales which the survivors had heard from their Indian captors, tales of Seven Cities of Gold, hidden somewhere in the folds of the great grassland in the north.

And so once more Spanish greed sent Spanish soldiers into the unknown.

Don Antonio Mendoza, Viceroy of all Mexico, had listened to these and other tales of adventure. Now he decided to find out the truth about the great continent which was known to exist in the north.

First, he sent out a small expedition led by a Franciscan friar. This little force penetrated the Yaqui mountains and reached the edge of the grasslands – the *despoblado*, they called them, a grassy desert stretching endlessly into the distance. Hidden somewhere in the folds of this open country, the Indian guides told the good Friar Marcos, was Cibola . . . 'with many streets and squares and

As the centuries went by the Spaniards imported more and more horses into New Spain. Here, Remington shows a Mexican vaquero, *forerunner of the modern cowboy, galloping out on a spirited horse. Many of these splendid beasts were lost during fighting with the Indians ; others strayed and founded the wild-horse herds which were to bring such a change to life on the plains. See the next page.*

7

*' The feather-streaming, buffalo-chasing, wild-
running, recklessly-fighting Indians of the
Plains' . . . ' the finest cavalry in the world' . . .
these are the sort of tributes that the white man
has paid to Indian horsemanship. Yet when the
Spaniards met them, the red men were a trudging
foot people, using dogs to carry their tents and
poles and belongings. But the plains were the best
breeding ground in the world and the gamma
grass, which dried in the winter to form a natural
hay on the root, served the stray horses which the
Spaniards lost or left there, as well as it served
the buffalo. Between 1500 and 1800 the stray
horses multiplied, and the Indians were not slow
to catch these new animals and turn them to their
own use. First the Comanche, then the Cheyenne,
the Apache, the Pawnee, the Sioux . . . the
' horse culture', as it was called, moved rapidly
north and transformed the Indians' whole way
of life. This painting of a buffalo hunt is by
Charles Russell.*

*The buffalo provided the Plains
Indian with almost everything
he needed. With the skins he
made his house, clothes, rope
and wool. The sinews were used
for sewing and for bowstrings,
the bones for tools. The bladders
became water containers and the
meat was dried in the sun,
pounded and mixed with berries
to make ' jerky' or pemmican
to eat during the winter. This
picture of the inside of an
Indian tepee was painted by
Karl Bodmer in 1833.*

houses eleven stories high, with fronts and doors of turquoise'.

Could this be the first of the fabled seven cities? The friar hurried back with the news.

The next expedition was a more formidable affair, designed to penetrate the *despoblado* itself, and was led by a man whose name was to echo through the epic of the discovery of the Great West.

Francisco Vasquez de Coronado rode out of Compostela one February day in 1540 at the head of 250 mounted troops, nearly 100 foot soldiers, several hundred friendly Indians, four priests – and Friar Marcos. *Remudas* of horses, herds of cattle, sheep and swine followed; a living larder for the march.

9

To the natives of the country the white soldiery appeared terrifying. They had never seen the gigantic beasts that were horses and men; they knew nothing of armour and musket. They melted before the expedition as it pressed up the narrow river valleys. Then, at last, the Spaniards reached the deserts and mesas of Arizona and the first of their fabled cities – Cibola.

Coronado's heart sank at the sight. For instead of a glittering Aztec city all aflash with jewels and gold, a mean pile of tenements, the stone and adobe buildings of the Pueblo Indians, rose before them. And drawn up to defend their homes with bows, arrows, shields and war clubs were some 300 or 400 Indians.

The Spaniards raised their war cry of 'Santiago', and stormed the town. It was a vast pyramid of buildings into which the desperate defenders retreated to hurl down stones and arrows upon the cavalry below. Coronado himself was carried from the field unconscious, his gilded helmet dented by the rain of rocks. But superior arms and discipline prevailed and 'Cibola', or the Zuni pueblo of Hawikuh, was taken.

The army wintered there in 1540–41. Friar Marcos was packed off back to Mexico, discredited, and Coronado anxiously questioned the natives in an effort to discover exactly what kind of people lived on the plains.

All the next summer the expedition probed north and east. They crossed the Pecos River; they met the Plains Indians and saw the vast herds of buffalo off which they lived; they reached the broad Arkansas River and made friends with the proud Wichita tribe. But they found no cities of gold; only a vast expanse of grass, rolling like an ocean ever northwards. Clouds piled high in the sky. The horizons shimmered in the heat. The men sweated in their armour and the horses hung their heads.

At length, frustrated and with another winter coming on, the Spaniards turned back. After two years in the wilderness the expedition stumbled across the Rio Grande into Mexico.

There had been little loss of life; the Commander still rode at the head of his men. And they had penetrated the Great West farther than any white man had done before. But the Coronado expedition was counted a costly failure. The dreams of finding another golden empire faded.

After this, only the cows of old Villalobos nosed north again.

The Spaniards now turned to their second target in the New World: to spread the influence of their church as far as they could.

Like the beams of a searchlight, the power of Spain probed north from Mexico. One beam pointed up the Pacific coast as far as San Francisco – Yerba Buena, they called it. Another penetrated the deep valley of the Colorado River. A third struck deep into the Pueblo country where Coronado had fought the Zunis. And a fourth beam swung north-east, towards that green triangle of land across which de Vaca and his companions had wandered, the great south-west of America which was to become the true home of the cowboy.

Into this cradle of the cattle kingdom came, first, the soldiers to subdue the Indians and to build forts, or *presidios*, for protection. Then the priests followed and, gradually, a chain of missions was established across the country. The one at San Jose, just south of

The Californian method of catching cattle ; Spanish vaqueros, *the first cowboys, in action in 1826. Note the* lasso *and the* tapaderos.

San Antonio, was typical. Two hundred Indians who had been converted to Christianity lived there.

Under the watchful eyes of the Franciscan friars they learned to farm until over 3,000 bushels of corn were produced in a year. Herds of sheep came north, and then cattle; descendants of those few beasts which had scrambled ashore from the ships of Villalobos, perhaps. And with them came the men the Spaniards had taught to tend the cows, the *vaqueros*.

Because the Indians in this plentiful land were friendly the Spaniards called them *tejas*, meaning 'allies' or 'friends', and so the country became known as 'the land of the Tejas', or Texas.

Poor, primitive and probably branded on the cheek with a G (for *guerra* — war) these *vaqueros* were the first cowboys and proud of their calling. They lived with the beasts they tended in lean-to shelters. Their diet was *atole* mush, a sort of corn-meal porridge.

The penetration of the Plains.

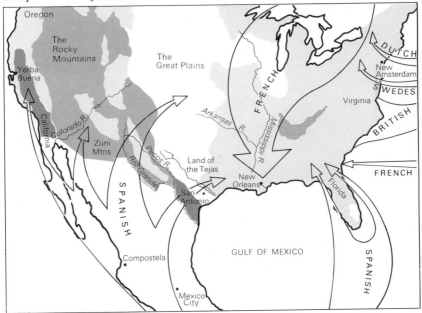

While the Spanish pushed north from the Rio Grande, other countries, too, were exploring the New World. The French took to the waterways — they called it la grande portage *— and came up the St Lawrence River, through the Great Lakes and then down the mighty Mississippi to the Gulf of Mexico. Frederic Remington painted this picture of one of their expeditions.*

They caught what game they could with their *reatas*, for their masters would not trust them with firearms.

When they could get them, they strapped the long, wicked Spanish spurs to their bare feet (for they could not afford boots). They could ride anything on four legs and would never walk if they could ride. They were very loyal to their herd and to their masters. In their hands, the *reata* became a fantastic weapon with which to throw the largest steer or catch the biggest stallion. Even, in a daring game played by three or four *vaqueros* together, trapping a bear and stretching the great roaring creature between them until the growls were choked and the fierce eyes dulled over in death.

In the land of the Tejas, these *vaqueros* learned to live alongside or fight with the Indians of the plains. And, as the centuries went by, their clothes, the tools of their trade, their customs and language and way of life passed into the world of the American cowboy.

Three hundred years went by, packed with tremendous events. While the Spaniards were busy building their Empire in the south, other European nations rushed to claim new lands. The English, the Dutch, the Swedes, the French . . . all these great migrations are shown on the map on page 12.

Each nation brought its own laws and language, as well as the material things needed to conquer the wilderness. Like tiny plants, small sprigs of Europe, the colonies took root and began to grow.

A fierce struggle to control the continent followed; French against English, Dutch against Swedes, with the Indians fighting on both sides. At last, tired of this squabbling, the colonists began to think of themselves as 'Americans', rather than descendants of faraway nations in Europe. They united and rebelled against the old world.

By the middle of the nineteenth century, the United States was one big country, and yet much of it was still a mystery.

From the Atlantic coast to the Mississippi and Missouri Rivers and all along the Pacific coastal plain there were settled lands, with farms and ranches, towns, roads and railways. In between the Rocky Mountains and the two great rivers the country was almost completely unexplored.

This was the *despoblado* which had defeated Coronado. A land of rolling grass, of blazing summer heat and vicious winter wind. Empty, save for a few wandering tribes and the vast herds of buffalo. They called it the Great American Desert or the Big Blue, a vast bowl of sky and prairie which the pioneers, heading for the lush climates of Oregon or California, strove to cross as quickly as possible. It was a useless land and nobody wanted it.

Until the cattlemen came.

Thousands of covered wagons crawled on to the Great Plains during the years 1840–60, heading west. To men and women used

The Language of the Range

Here are some of the words you would hear a cowboy use, even today. You will find many of them in your dictionary although they were originally Spanish. The American cowboy took them from the *vaqueros*; kept some of them as pure Spanish, twisted others to suit his own purpose. The way to pronounce some of the words is shown in brackets.

Bronco (bron′-ko). Spanish for wild, rough. The name given to any small, spirited horse.

Adobe (a-dōbee). Spanish for clay. Usually refers to sun-dried brick.

Chaparejos (sha′-pa-ra′-hoes). Mexican-Spanish for leather leggings, worn as protection against thorny bushes. Called 'chaps', for short.

Chaparral (sha′-pa-rol′). Spanish for dense thicket of brush or thorny trees.

Cinch (sinch). Spanish 'cincha', a wide strap with rings at the end which passes under a horse's belly and holds the saddle on.

Corral (ko-ral′). Spanish for fenced yard for animals.

Hacienda (hah-see-en′-dah). Spanish for farm with big house as headquarters.

Honda (hon′-dah). The metal or leather oval at the end of a lariat which makes a free-running noose.

Latigo (la-tee′-go). The strap which comes down from the saddle to slip into the cinch ring.

La reata (ray-ah′- tah). Spanish for rope. Cowboys turned it into 'lariat'.

Lasso. Spanish for a noose.

Mesa (may′-sah). Spanish for table. Used to describe a flat-topped plateau.

Pinto (peen′-tow). Spanish for painted; thus a painted or spotted horse.

Pueblo (pweb′-low). Spanish for village. Usually an Indian village in cowboy parlance.

Rancho (ran′-cho). Spanish for ranch.

Remuda (ray-mew′-dah). Spanish for a group or string of horses.

Sombrero (som-brer′-oh). Wide-brimmed Spanish hat with tall crown.

Tapadero (tă-pâ-day′-ro). The hood over the stirrup which protects a cowboy's foot. Shortened to 'taps'.

Vaquero (vah-kair′-oh). From the Spanish word 'vaca' – a cow. Means a cow-herder.

Da la vuelta. This Spanish phrase is for the action of wrapping the end of a lariat round the saddle horn when roping an animal in order to throw it. The cowboys twisted it to 'dolly welter' and, eventually, to 'dolly' or 'dally' (see page 37).

to friendly hills, trees and green meadows, embarking on the westward trail seemed like sailing out of a sheltered port on to the open sea. The summer-browned grass stretched endlessly away on either side of the narrow wagon track; there was nothing familiar about the monotonous plain or wind-scarred butte. Little wonder they thought of the country as a desert and were anxious to grasp the first helping hand held out to them on the trail.

The pioneers brought with them their own horses and cattle to stock the farms they would build once they had crossed the mountains. But by the time the wagons were rolling along the North Platte River the animals were footsore and weary, and often stores would be running low. When the caravan stopped at a river crossing or trading post, the weak dairy cows from the soft Missouri valleys would be exchanged for a few dollars or some sacks of flour.

Gradually, ranches sprang up along the trail, where traders relieved the pioneers of their worn-out cattle and then proceeded to fatten them up in the grassy valleys. Later on, they would be exchanged – at a profit, of course – with the next bunch of travellers who wanted fresh animals to complete their journey.

The first great wave of western migration went along the Oregon Trail in the mid 80s and spread a ripple of disaster over the prairie. For, although the pioneers themselves left the buffalo undisturbed, the hunters were soon to follow and, in a brief orgy of killing, swept the huge herds from the plains. Painting by W. H. D. Koerner.

The long trip to the west was far from the easy adventure that films sometimes make it out to be. Look closely at this old picture of a family on the Oregon Trail, at the bare feet and skimpy clothes of the children and the rickety, old wagons. These were the real pioneers.

So it was, in this small way, that the cattlemen first broke the myth of the Great American Desert and proved that cattle, like the buffalo, could prosper on the plains.

Meanwhile, in the south-west, an important change had taken place. The Mexicans, who had so successfully colonized California and the 'land of the Tejas', lost these great areas of land in a brief war with the United States. The herds of cattle, which first the Spanish missions and then the Mexican *ranchos* had done so much to establish, were left to their own devices by the retreating *vaqueros*. The aggressive Texas settlers, coming into the rich, pastoral land around the River Neuces, found so many cattle that they did not bother to brand the newly-dropped calves.

There was little demand for all this beef. A small trade grew up along the Gulf coast in hides, tallow, hoof and horn; the carcasses of Texas steers providing leather, candles and glue for the rest of the United States. Then, as the Texans looked desperately around for a market for this potential wealth-on-the-hoof, the Civil War broke out.

The cowboys joined the Southern Confederacy, and for four long years fought a losing battle against the north. Attempts were made to supply beef to the fighting army by driving herds to New Orleans and the Mississippi towns. But when northern soldiers fought their way right down the river valley to the sea, Texas was cut off from the rest of the southern states.

The longhorns roamed through the lush valleys, untended, and when the Texas cowboys came home from the war they reckoned there were more than five million of them. For the ugly beast had a very long and tough ancestry.

The Texas longhorn was a direct descendant of the rough, lanky, long-horned Spanish animal originally reared in large herds by the Moors on the plains of Andalusia.

When the Civil War broke out, vast areas of America were devastated by the fighting. Farms and ranches were burned; cattle were left to their own devices or driven off to feed the rival armies.

Everything about him was long – long body, long legs, long tail and, above all, tremendous horns. They swept out on either side of his head in a wide curve; up and out again towards a white and blue polished tip as sharp as a Spanish stiletto. Sometimes, old steers carried horns measuring seven feet (two metres) from tip to tip. At their base near the head they became crinkled and cracked like the bark on a tree, which sometimes caused the cowboys to call them 'mossy horns'. In colour, the longhorn was anything from yellow or red, to dun or black – and sometimes a mixture of all those colours with an iron grey streak down the side as well.

As this weird-looking animal spread northwards with the slowly advancing Spanish settlements, it developed extraordinary endurance. It could stand extremes of heat and cold; it could climb like a goat; it could live for a long time without water, and it would eat almost anything that grew.

When the Texas settlers moved in to the old Mexican colonies they brought with them their own domesticated cattle, descendants in their turn from the red Devon cows and yellow Danish oxen which had landed at the early Atlantic coast settlements. The strains of the south-west and the east were mingled, giving the longhorn heavier bone, better flesh. But the underlying quality of toughness remained.

Which was a good thing, because he had a long way to go!

Until now, the longhorn's home had been the ideal cattle country of de Vaca's wanderings; the country where snow and ice came rarely; where there was water enough for good grass but not enough for trees; where cattle could drift from feeding ground to feeding ground unhindered.

Most of these wandering longhorns were 'mavericks', cattle without owners, which could be claimed by anyone who cared to round them up and put a brand on them.

In this country, too, were herds of wild horses, a great store of mustangs which, since the times of the Spaniards, had provided Indian and cowboy alike with mounts.

Grass – water – cattle – horses . . . it needed only one more thing –

men. And the returning soldiers would provide that. The cattle industry was about to explode!

The Texans came home to a poor state; farms and industries had been allowed to run down, Confederate money was now useless. About the only assets they had were the 5,000,000 long-horns. But even at $3 or $4 a head for branded stock there was nobody to buy them.

In the north it was very different. The northern states, the Union, had won the war largely because of their industries. They had been able to build the heavy guns, which gave them power over the south; they had fed their soldiers better, even making experiments with dried or dessicated foods, canned milk and canned beef. But all this had not been done without some cost. The livestock had almost disappeared from the upper Missouri valley, taken by the beef packers to feed the army. In Chicago, there were big stockyards where cattle were slaughtered and then shipped east on the new railroads. But these stockyards were empty, and owners like P. D. Armour and G. F. Swift were ready to pay $30 or $40 a head for cattle to keep their factories working. In a word, the North was hungry. It didn't take the South long to find this out.

During the winter of 1865-6 the Texans went to work, rounding up cattle, building wagons to carry camp equipment and cooking stoves, hiring cowboys at $25 to $40 a month for the 'long drive' north.

At that time, the railroads had barely reached the edge of the prairie. There were great plans to lay a line right across the continent and intense rivalry between grandly-named railroad companies to be the first to do so. But that winter the track-laying gangs were still in the forests of Missouri.

The Texans aimed for Sedalia; a little town just south of the Missouri River and the railhead of the Missouri–Pacific Railroad Company. From there a line ran east to the large city of St Louis on the Mississippi.

In March, when the grass on the northern range began to grow, the first 'long drive' started. About a dozen herds – 260,000 head in all – set off steadily north, but it proved to be far from an easy

The Texas cowboys came back to a ruined State, but there was one good sight to greet them — the vast herds of cattle which had multiplied during the years the men had been away fighting. In the north, beef was in short supply . . . so the great cattle drives began. Painting by James Walker.

venture! Heavy rains muddied the ground. Beyond the Red River, Indians stampeded the herds and then demanded a reward for returning the longhorns to their owners. When they reached the wooded hills of the Ozark Plateau the steers baulked at the unfamiliar sight of trees and had to be whipped through the woods.

Farther on, angry farmers came out, fearing that the cattle would trample down their crops and shooting the leaders when they failed to stop. To make matters worse, bands of outlaws (they were called 'jayhawkers' or 'redlegs', after the red strip down the military trousers that many still wore) turned on the cowboys and attempted to rob the herds.

The 'long drive' of '66 was far from a success. But the steers which *did* reach Sedalia were sold for $35 a head; that seemed to be a convincing reason for persevering, if a safer trail could be found.

In fact, Jesse Chisholm had already found that safer trail a couple of years before, when he brought a wagon load of buffalo hides up across the Red and Canadian Rivers, and the Salt Fork and the Cimarron to Wichita, in Kansas – the land that Coronado had reached so long ago. It was farther west than the Texans liked and it ran through Indian territory, but then Jesse was a half-breed Cherokee and travelled among friends.

The following year he drove a small herd north and marked the trail for future use. He marked it simply: by throwing up a mound of earth every few miles, an outstanding feature against a flat skyline. It was to become the most famous trail of them all.

Marking out the Chisholm Trail coincided with the bright idea of an Illinois cattle dealer named Joseph M. McCoy – the 'real McCoy'. He realized that, somewhere, southern cowboys and northern buyers had to meet. The best place, he reckoned, was out on the prairie where there were no settlements or trees to hinder the northward-rolling herds.

He made a contract for favourable freight rates with two railroad companies, the Kansas Pacific, already building out on the plains, and the Hannibal and St Joe Railroad, who had tracks running back to Chicago.

In the spring of 1867, at a well-grassed, well-watered little town called Abilene, McCoy unloaded trainload after trainload of timber. Timber for stockyards, pens and loading chutes. Timber for barns, stables, stores . . . and for a big hotel for the trail-stained cowboys. And while the hammers and saws were still busy he sent riders hurrying south to meet the northbound herds with news of the new market.

Keeping a herd moving up the trail was a tough job. Every day called for action – and plenty of it! As soon as it was light enough to see, the cattle, who had been bedded down in a big circle, would be prodded into a pear-shaped mass by all the riders of the outfit. On three sides they would press in, whooping, and the lead steers – those who plodded naturally to the head of the line every morning – would push through to the open side and lead out onto the trail broken by the chuck wagon, rolling a mile or so ahead.

The herd would then string out, perhaps a mile or more in

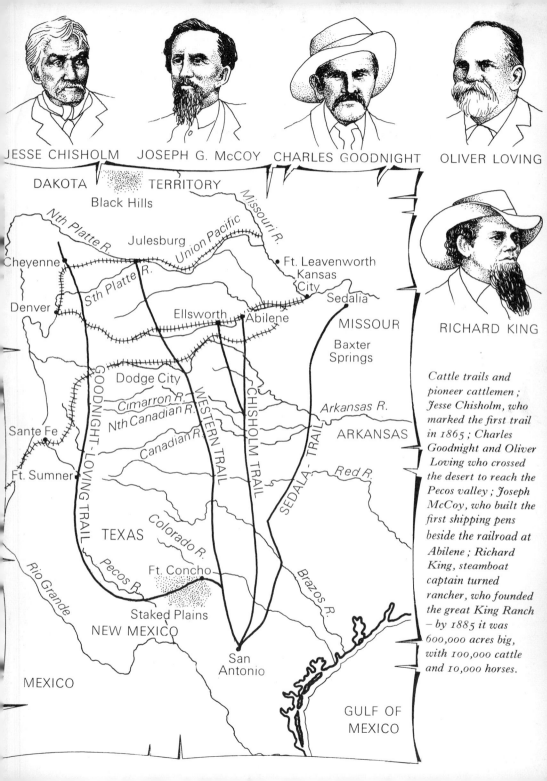

JESSE CHISHOLM JOSEPH G. McCOY CHARLES GOODNIGHT OLIVER LOVING

RICHARD KING

DAKOTA TERRITORY

Black Hills

Nth Platte R.

Julesburg

Missouri R.

Union Pacific

Cheyenne

Sth Platte R.

Ft. Leavenworth
Kansas
City

Denver

Ellsworth Abilene

Sedalia

MISSOUR

Baxter
Springs

Dodge City

Cimarron R.

Nth Canadian R.

Arkansas R.

ARKANSAS

Sante Fe

Canadian R.

Ft. Sumner

Red R.

TEXAS

Colorado R.

GOODNIGHT - LOVING TRAIL

WESTERN TRAIL

CHISHOLM TRAIL

SEDALA - TRAIL

Rio Grande

Pecos R.

Ft. Concho

Brazos R.

Staked Plains

NEW MEXICO

San
Antonio

MEXICO

GULF OF
MEXICO

*Cattle trails and
pioneer cattlemen;
Jesse Chisholm, who
marked the first trail
in 1865; Charles
Goodnight and Oliver
Loving who crossed
the desert to reach the
Pecos valley; Joseph
McCoy, who built the
first shipping pens
beside the railroad at
Abilene; Richard
King, steamboat
captain turned
rancher, who founded
the great King Ranch
– by 1885 it was
600,000 acres big,
with 100,000 cattle
and 10,000 horses.*

length. At point, two riders would keep the longhorns on their course; other cowboys guarded the flanks, or took over the role of swing riders when the column had to be turned. At the back came the drag, the laziest steers of them all, spread out in a slow-moving mass that had to be prodded continually by a line of riders eating the dust behind.

At noon, they would reach the halted chuck wagon where the cookie would have dinner waiting. The cattle grazed while the men ate; then on they would all go until nightfall. Throughout the hours of darkness the cowboys would take turns to ride herd, two at a time. And the same pattern would be repeated the next day.

It was a way of life that called for all the skills in the handling of cattle passed on by the old *vaqueros*. It demanded a steady, single-mindedness of purpose. And, above all, it demanded courage.

There were rivers to cross, broken country to negotiate and the ever-present threats of Indian attack or prairie storm. Little wonder that after months of hard riding and lonely living, the cowboys let out a 'yippee' of approval when they saw McCoy's new stockyards – and hotel!

With Abilene began the epic period of the Wild West. Between 1868 and 1871 nearly 1,500,000 Texas longhorns passed through the yards. The railroads pushed on across the Great Plains and other towns sprang up: Newton, Ellsworth, Dodge City . . . the 'cow towns' that would catapult the Texas cowboy into the lime-light. But before they were built there were two more famous drives to record.

Wyoming is the land of the high plains. Where the ground slopes eastwards from the Rocky Mountains, up near the North

Point 'em north! *One of Erwin E. Smith's magnificent photographs of Texas longhorns on the trail. They had a thousand miles to go – or more – before they reached the railheads.*

25

Positions of riders:–

P = Point
S = Swing
F = Flank
C = Counter
D = Drag

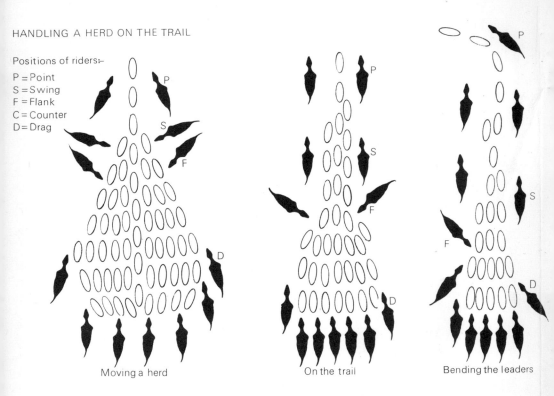

Moving a herd   On the trail   Bending the leaders

Platte and Laramie rivers, is a fine country of well-grassed bench land. The early pioneers, struggling towards Oregon, stopped to admire the rolling country, so different from the flat prairies. 'Wonderful soil,' said the farmers, kicking the dark ground with a worn heel. 'Fine cattle country,' said the stockmen, watching the wagon teams belly-deep in wild hay.

Then a shrill cry from their scouts and a long line of Sioux warriors on the horizon would send them scurrying back to their wagons.

By 1866 the Sioux had retreated north to the Powder River country and the *Cheyenne Daily Leader* was talking about raising cattle on the high plains. It took ten years for the dream to come true.

Checking a stampede   Holding stock   Counting cattle

But the possibility of stocking the Wyoming ranges with Texas cattle was demonstrated early on. Oliver Loving had been a trail driver during the Civil War. He'd been up the Sedalia Trail in 1858 and seen the herds stopped by raiders on the Kansas–Missouri border.

Charlie Goodnight had been in the cattle business all his life, too, and had the idea that new markets for Texas beef could be found in New Mexico and Colorado – if the longhorns could be pushed across the Staked Plains to the Pecos River.

The two men gathered a herd of 2,000 head, built one of the first chuck wagons, recruited Confederate army veterans as their crew, and pointed the herd *west*!

The first leg of the journey was a terrible 96 miles (about 150

Moving into Kansas in the summer of 1866, the cowboys were met by farmers who feared the cattle would trample their crops. Thieves and raiders, lawbreakers spawned by the Civil War, moved in on the halted herds. This painting by Charles Russell shows two horse thieves caught by a posse. He called the picture When Horseflesh Comes High.

kilometres) dry drive across the desert. The longhorns moved steadily, a brown stream on the white plain. There was little noise, the ground muffled the trampling hoofs and the riders were silent, masked against the choking alkali dust. Day and night they went on, eking out the water from the wagon among men and horses, leaving the longhorns to pant at the bare ground.

They climbed to a rough, rocky plateau; descended to soft, sinking sand. They shot the steers who got trapped in the salty sink holes; manhandled the wagon sometimes axle deep through the more dangerous patches. And all the time they dreaded the appearance of the wild Comanche out of the shimmering horizon on their right.

By the fourth day the longhorns were almost at their last gasp. Their ribs stuck out, their tongues were swollen and protruding. They moaned as they staggered on.

When they reached Castle Gap and smelled the Pecos they still had strength enough to stampede . . . until the river itself brought them to a halt.

Weaker cattle could never have done it. The longhorn's famed stamina had brought them through.

The partners rested for a few days and then made a count. They had lost 300 head in the desert. They pushed on north to Fort Sumner in New Mexico and sold the rest at a profit.

The Goodnight-Loving Trail had been opened.

The longest drive of them all was made by Nelson Story, a miner who had found gold in Montana. Hearing of the profits that could be made by buying cheaply in Texas and selling at the railheads, he went south early in 1866 with $10,000 sewn into the linings of his clothes.

At Fort Worth in Texas he collected a herd of about 1,000 longhorns, hired a crew, and set off. At Baxter Springs he was halted by jayhawkers and Kansas farmers. Instead of trying to fight his way through, Story remembered the shortage of good beef in the days he had spent in the north-west mining camps, and decided to head for Montana.

The herd turned west and moved leisurely along the Oregon Trail to Fort Laramie. There, the cowboys learned that the Sioux were on the warpath, attacking anything that moved along the route to the goldfields.

Quietly, Story bought twenty-five new Remington rapid-fire rifles, one for every man of his crew, and went on. At Fort Phil Kearny, virtually under siege by Red Cloud's army, the fort commandant told him firmly that the road was closed; he ordered Story to corral his herd close by the fort.

Story was in a fix and he knew it. If he delayed, the snows would soon close the trail completely. Forced to winter at the fort, he would have to pay off his crew and sell the cattle to the army – at prices far below those they would fetch in the goldfields!

Secretly, round the campfire on the night of 21 October, Story asked his men to vote: should they disobey the order and push on up the dangerous trail . . . or stay put? Only one man voted 'Stay'.

Next morning, cowboys and herd had vanished – taking with them at gun point the one protesting rider who could have given the game away. Trailing by night, grazing by day, beating off the Indian attacks, the determined herd pushed on. At last, on 9 December, Story led 600 head of cattle into the goldfields near Virginia City. They had travelled nearly 2,000 miles (3,200 kilometres), the longest cattle drive in the history of the West.

At the end of a trail, a cowboy would have ridden well over a thousand miles (1,600 kilometres) looking after his charges. He would also have spent many months without ever getting a full night's sleep. The bed, when he did hit it, was bare ground; the pillow, a saddle – unless he had to use it as a shelter to keep off hail-

At railheads like Abilene, the herds were held in great pens until they could be loaded onto special trains. Cracking long whips, the cowboys urged the cattle into the cars. Drawing of Abilene by Henry Worrall.

stones as big as ping-pong balls if the weather turned bad! He might have fought off Indians trying to steal the horses; spent sixty hours in the saddle at one stretch, looking for cattle scattered by a stampede; even fought prairie fires.

It was small wonder, then, that when the herd was sold and the trail boss rode into camp with the pay roll, all hell broke loose. With a fistful of money in one hand and a smoking six-shooter in the other, the cowboy would 'yippee' down the trail in a cloud of dust, bent on waking up the town.

And it was in the cow towns that the legend of the 'wild' west really began. They were dismal hamlets most of the time, a few scattered streets of mean shacks where bored traders whiled away the weeks between the arrival of each herd. But when the cowboys did come, the town leaped to noisy life, and respectable citizens watched the whirling ponies and wild young men from behind barred doors and shuttered windows.

At night, the saloons gleamed with light. Gambling dens,

The great engine – perhaps a wood burner with a fat smoke stack – would pull out, bell clanging, longhorns bellowing, heading east to the meat markets.

hurdy-gurdy palaces, gaudy dance halls throbbed with activity until the sun rose. In a few short days and nights the gamblers and dance hall girls relieved the cowboys of the money that they had worked so many months to earn. There would be bar-room brawls, drunken duels and shooting demonstrations to impress the visitors from the east. And, more often than not, one of the crew would be left up on 'Boot Hill', the local cemetery reserved for those who 'died with their boots on'.

Each railhead, from Baxter Springs to Dodge City had a short, riotous life. Each town, in turn, claimed the title of 'the wildest town in the west'.

But it must not be forgotten that the cowboys creating such havoc at the end of the long drive were young men letting off steam after months of hard work. There were also desperadoes, it is true, whose adventures would fill another book. And as lawlessness grew, the citizens of the cow towns banded together to hire a marshall tough enough to tame the cowboys.

Tom Smith was the first marshall of Abilene; he used his fists, not a six-gun, to put respect for the law into the minds of boisterous cowhands. James B. Hickok (Wild Bill) was his successor and an amazing marksman. There was Pat Garrett, who captured Billy the Kid; Bill Tilghman, who took the notorious train robber, Bill Doolin, single-handed. And, moving from Ellsworth, to Wichita, to Dodge City and then Tombstone, the legendary Wyatt Earp.

But tales grow in the telling. The 'battle' of the O.K. Corral, as it is so often called, lasted little more than a minute and only about thirty shots were fired. This is not to detract from the courageous job that these lawmen did. But the romantic picture of the cowboy as a two-fisted, gun-slinging hell-raiser is only a tiny part of the story. For the most he was a steady worker on a spirited horse, doing a long, lonely job.

The adventures of the Texas cowboys all combined to push the cattleman's frontier deeper and deeper into the Great Plains. No longer did people think of the country between the Rocky Mountains and the Mississippi River as a 'desert'. The myth of the *despoblado*, as the Spaniards had christened it, began to fade

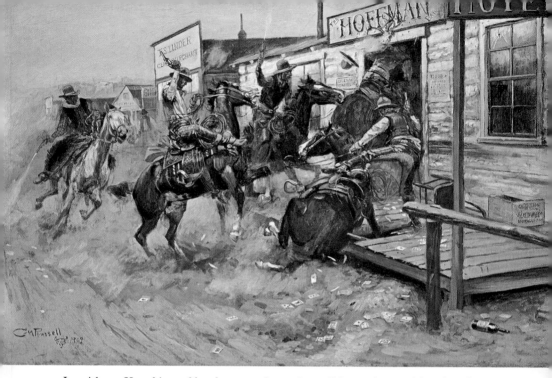

In without Knocking. *After long months on the trail it wasn't surprising that the cowboys let off steam once the cattle were pastured and they drew their pay. The railhead towns became notorious for their rowdyism and lawlessness. Charles Russell painted this picture of cowboys having a little fun at Glendive, in Montana, in 1881.*

even when the first cowboy drove the first longhorn into the sea of grass.

The rivalry between the railroad companies, racing to be the first to cross the continent, pushed the railheads farther west each year. There were perhaps a dozen of them, including the Union Pacific, the Kansas Pacific, the Atchison, Topeka and Sante Fe, the Burlington, the Texas Pacific. And as the cow towns blossomed on the prairie the Indians retreated, the buffalo were killed off and the whole country was transformed.

For once the first flush of money-making excitement was over and Texas began to recover from the effects of the Civil War,

33

both northern buyers and southern cattlemen took a hard look at the scene.

The long drive meant at least 1,500 miles of solid walking over an arduous trail. The cattle lost weight; and before they could fetch the high prices that their owners wanted they had to be fattened up on grain. And that was expensive.

There were other troubles, too. Once the tracks were laid, railroad companies wanted an income from the trains running over them every day, not just when the long drive reached its end. So to encourage settlers to build farms near the shining rails they offered them land at very cheap rates. And soon, like the farmers around Baxter Springs in the early days of the cattle drives, the prairie farmers feared that Texas cattle would trample down their crops and bring Texas fever into the area. In the tough hide of the

Shootings were frequent. This is a famous sketch by Remington of a gunfight in the street.

Many a tenderfoot got his first initiation into the ways of the west with an invitation to 'Dance!' as the bullets chipped the ground around his feet.

longhorn lived a tick which could carry disease, and although the longhorn itself might be immune, the tick could fall off and attach itself to the next cow that passed. This might well be an animal from the new farm, not nearly so tough as the Texas breed, and it wasn't long before quarantine laws were passed to stop the longhorns entering the new settlements.

The Indians, too, who had been granted land on the prairie by the Government, began to charge the cowboys a toll of 10 cents a head to bring the longhorns across their reservations.

In the face of this growing opposition, the cattleman changed his tactics. If he could no longer drive his cattle north from the old breeding grounds in Texas, then he must 'grow' his cattle out on the prairie, close to the railroads. He knew that the climate could be harsh, with winter gales and ice storms, but he also knew that the longhorns had proved their toughness on the Goodnight-Loving Trail and with Nelson Story in Wyoming. Turned loose on the Great Plains they could scrape away the snow in the winter to find the natural, cured hay that had kept the buffalo going, and fatten up in the spring. If it blew a blizzard, then they could just turn their boney rumps to the wind and drift before it.

So the longhorns were turned loose and it wasn't long before great ranches dotted the plains from the Rio Grande Valley to the Big Horn Mountains.

About this time, too, things were happening back east to help the cattleman. The stockyards and slaughter houses were being modernized; refrigerator wagons had been invented for the railroads, and cold storage plants built at the depots. Even the stringy longhorn meat was changed; toughness on the trail was all right but nobody wanted it on the plate!

The English breeders began to take an interest in the western cattle industry. They shipped over Hereford and Angus bulls to breed with the native cattle. The result was a round-bellied, white-faced animal, which had the longhorn's stamina but the weight and tenderness of the English breeds. The new cattle could survive the winter, roam contented in the summer, and fetch high prices in the stockyards. Soon the western range was supplying meat for all eastern America and much of Europe, too.

Maybe it was in a can, but those old Andalusian herds were coming home!

State	Cattle in 1860	Cattle in 1880
Kansas	93,455	1,533,133
Nebraska	37,197	1,113,247
Colorado	None	791,492
Wyoming	None	521,213
Montana	None	428,279
Dakota	None	140,815

R. A. Billington, *Westward Expansion*, New York: The Macmillan Co., 1960.

By 1880, a cowboy riding north from Texas would seldom be out of sight of the white-faced longhorns. He would find many fences across his path, now, and curse the 'Bob wire', as he contemptuously called it. But the blooded stock had to be separated from the old, wild longhorns and this new invention, with its wicked barbs, enabled the rancher to close off his own breed. From the Staked Plains to New Mexico, from Kansas to Colorado, from

In A Tight Dally and a Loose Latigo *Russell has recorded a common enough range-life mishap. The 'dally' was the hitch the cowboy took around his saddle horn after roping a steer; the 'latigo' was the strap that held his saddle on. When one was tight and the other loose, the cowboy was in trouble!*

Dakota to Montana the cowboy had created a new empire, the Cattle Kingdom of the American West.

Statistics are sometimes dull, but the table opposite shows how big things became in just twenty years.

The day of the cowboy had reached its noon. Now's the time to look at the man who had made it all possible.

The word 'cowboy' was first used to describe the men of New York State who made a trade of stealing cattle during the American Revolution. Then, when Texas broke away from Mexico, the Texans who rustled cattle from across the Rio Grande were also

In 1894, a young lad of eight named Erwin Smith began working on the JSC ranch near Quanah, Texas. The cowboys ignored his youth and treated him like a regular cowhand. He resolved to become an authority on the west and. later, began experi-

called 'cowboys'. It was many years before the word became the respectable, romantic term for the rider of the plains.

The cowboy was a Texas phenomenon. In thirty short years, roughly from 1860 to 1890, he spread the techniques that he had learned from the *vaquero* all over the Great Plains. These techniques changed slightly, of course, depending on where he went. For instance, a short rope was used in mountain or brush country; a long one on the open plain. But the buckaroo, waddie, bronc buster, cowpuncher or whatever he was called (never cattleman — that referred to the owner) was the same man, whether his home range was in Montana or New Mexico, a copy of the original Texan.

The cowboy world, as far as numbers went, was a small one. Nobody knows how many cowboys there were; a few thousands, perhaps, for one cowboy could take care of a great number of cows and cover a vast area. In the days of the big ranches it was nothing for a cowboy to go a hundred miles to *get* to his work.

menting with a box camera. In 1905 Smith set out for some of the biggest ranches in the south-west and began to take some of the first – and finest – photographs of life on the range. Above, a group of cowboys ride in for the evening meal.

He was usually single and, because he spent so much of his time alone with his horse, accustomed to silence and famed for expressing himself in a few words.

And although he was paid a regular wage he was very independent, never thinking of himself as a 'hired hand'. He was very loyal to his outfit and to the cattle in his care; physical danger was something he had to live with every day and he took this with a shrug of his shoulders, as part of the job.

The cowboy was very dependent on his horse and had a great affection for it, although the mount usually belonged to the outfit for which he worked.

The finely-tooled leather saddle which he threw on its back was a direct descendant of the large wooden Spanish saddle. It had a high cantle, or back, and a horn in front so that the rider sat deep and could not slide off whatever his horse did. Leather strings hung from it to secure his blankets, canteen and waterproof slicker;

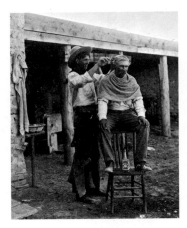

Smith called the series of photographs from which these on the right were taken, The Usual Morning Fight. *The western cow pony, even when trained, was often 'spooky' and not inclined to accept the saddle meekly. The fight was likely to be repeated three or four times a day as the cowboy changed mounts so as not to overwork the* remuda, *or saddle horses.*

Left : even cowboys had to have their hair cut!

everything was tied down. The saddle was single or double rigged – that is, with one cinch or two – depending on the way the cowboy roped. With a single rig he would rope dally style, lassoing his steer and taking a turn of the long rope round the saddle horn to throw it. With Texas hard-and-fast style roping, he would lasso the steer at close quarters and then jump his mount away at right angles so that the shock would pull the beast over, very often in a somersault. This technique demanded two cinches to keep the saddle on – a double rig.

The saddle was the cowboy's own property. It was often lavishly and lovingly decorated for it was in this seat, on top of a running, twisting, jumping, bucking 900 lb (about 400 kilogramme) horse, that a cowboy's work was done. This part of his equipment just had to be the best, to stand the strain put upon it. During round-up a cowboy would throw hundreds of steers, leaping off to hog-tie them before they could rise, then jumping into the saddle again to go after the next beast, while the branding teams moved among the prostrate animals with their smoking irons.

The cowboy rode with legs at full stretch, not in the English style with knees bent. His stirrups were sometimes covered with leather 'taps', to protect his feet. Like the old *vaquero*, the cowboy prided himself on being able to ride anything on four legs and to rope anything that ran on the range.

A round-up camp centred on the chuck wagon.
This was an ordinary lumber wagon with a stack of
boxes or compartments built at the back. In these
were stored sugar, spices, coffee, baking powder . . .
all the 'cookie's' necessities. A sloping lid opened
backwards and, with a hinged leg, made a table at
which he could work. Water barrels were slung on
each side and water drawn off each in turn so as
not to upset the balance of the wagon. Into the
wagon bed went the sacks of provisions, the pots
and pans and the cowboys' bed rolls. Underneath,
was a 'cooney' – a sagging cowhide tied at the four
corners; into this were thrown sticks and dried
buffalo chips as the wagon rolled along. These
provided fuel for the fire, which was generally
made in a pit to minimize the danger of setting the
prairie grass alight. A Dutch Oven was a big, cast-
iron pan with a flanged lid. Coals from the sloping
end of the pit could be shovelled on to the top to
speed the cooking.

To hold the remuda, two lariats were run out
from the wheels of the wagon to form a corral. In
the open end, a saddled horse was often left, with
reins trailing. In this position a trained cow pony
would not move from the spot and would prevent
others from straying.

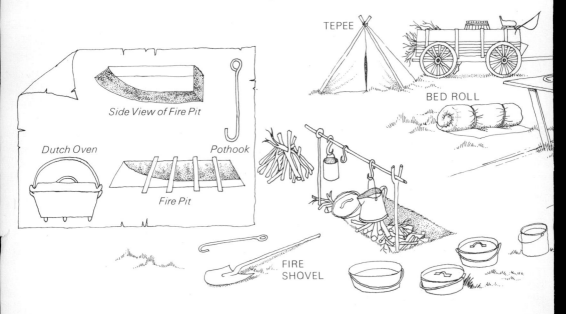

Side View of Fire Pit

Dutch Oven
Pothook
Fire Pit

TEPEE

BED ROLL

FIRE
SHOVEL

There was a reason for everything he wore, from the high heeled boots – probably designed to keep his feet from slipping out of the stirrups – to the crown of his hat – a 'John B', named after the man who made them, John B. Stetson. The high crown of the hat kept the sun from his head and the four-inch (100 mm.) brim kept it out of his eyes. The 'John B' was absolutely water-proof, kept out the rain, hail and snow and could be tied down over the ears when the thermometer plummeted below zero. It was wash bowl and drinking bowl for man and mount.

Between hat and boots everything had to fit snug and tight so as not to get in the way when the cowboy was working in the saddle. The bandana round his neck acted as a mask in dust storms, a bandage, tourniquet, or a horse hobble in an emergency. Shirts had collars attached; vests or waistcoats, sometimes of leather but usually cloth, provided useful pockets and left his arms free. Gloves, never worn for appearance, nor to keep his hands warm, prevented the cowboy from burning himself on a sliding rope.

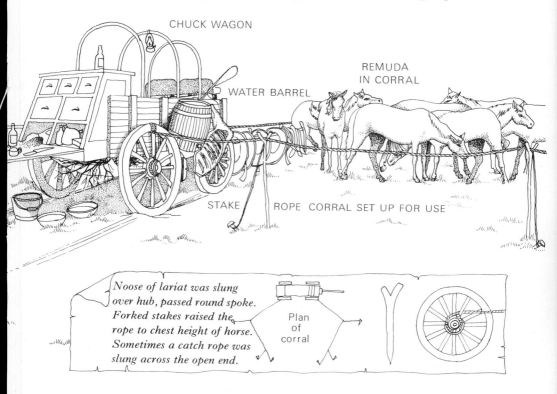

CHUCK WAGON

REMUDA
IN CORRAL

WATER BARREL

STAKE   ROPE CORRAL SET UP FOR USE

Noose of lariat was slung over hub, passed round spoke. Forked stakes raised the rope to chest height of horse. Sometimes a catch rope was slung across the open end.

Plan
of
corral

The cowboy's life was not all sunshine. Often, it was a tough, lonely life. Sixty hours in the saddle holding a herd that's trying all the time to stampede; mending fences in winter, blue with cold and muffled up to the eyebrows. This painting, by W. H. D. Koerner, shows one of the grimmer sides of things. It could have been the winter of 1886. That year, the greatest blizzard in the history of the west hit South Dakota and blew for eleven days. A knife-edge gale swept ice and snow over the level plains as far south as Texas. The thermometer plummeted; the herds could do nothing except turn their tails to the storm and drift with it. Cowboys froze to their saddles. Cattle perished by the thousands in the rivers and against the fences. It was the biggest 'die-up' ever, and long years were needed for the cattle industry to recover from this terrible blow.

His trousers were blue denim, originally made by a tailor called Levi Strauss, whose name was adopted, like Stetson's, for his product. And over these levis the cowboy wore 'chaps'.

These were a sort of leather armour which protected his legs from thorny bush and cactus. 'Shot-gun' chaps were like a pair of drain-pipe trousers without a seat. The legs were separate and joined by a belt at the top. 'Bat wing' chaps had a large flap on the

W. H. D
Koerner
1 9 3 1

outside which protected the horse's flank, and the cowboy liked them because they could be snapped on without taking off his spurs. In the north, 'woollies' or 'Angoras' were worn, made from sheep or goat skin to give the extra warmth needed in the winter.

Finally, the cowboy wore a gun. It was usually a Colt revolver, which was first used by the Texas Rangers in the war against Mexico in 1846. Its popularity then spread to the rider on the

Gradually the free range vanished. The railroads offered cheap land for settlement and Joseph L. Glidden's new, patented barbed wire enabled the farmer to fence his fields cheaply; the rancher to prevent his stock from roaming and to keep his water holes for his own use. The west became divided into 'fence men' and 'free-range men'. Here, small farmers, masked against recognition, cut the wire which cattlemen have used to fence off their water supply. But the 'fence men' won. By the turn of the century the range saw the first of the bonanza farms, with squadrons of ploughs and reapers moving across the waving grass. The day of the cowboy was almost over.

plains. He carried it as a tool of his trade, just like a farmer carried a walking stick. He used it against wild life, against ferocious cattle, against Indians. And he crushed his coffee beans with its butt! A whole book of lore has grown up around the 'fast gun' and the 'quick draw'. They did happen, of course; but the average cowboy probably went through his whole life without ever firing his gun at another man.

This, then, was the man who conquered the Great Plains.

The world got to know him when Owen Wister wrote *The Virginian* – just about the first western story. He's still riding today as 'Shane' or 'Monte Walsh', in a host of fine films and stories.

He came on the stage as the pioneers left. It had taken hundreds of years to prepare the scene for him. Yet the day of the cowboy was a short one, perhaps thirty years at the most.

46

His daily round was a tough one, it varied little and he performed it often alone. Herding, roping, branding, night guarding, trail driving. It was nothing for a cowboy to spend eighteen out of twenty-four hours in the saddle, no matter what the weather. As a rough string rider, he broke the mean horses for his outfit. As a rep or stray man, he worked with neighbouring outfits to claim the stock belonging to his own ranch. As a horse wrangler or jingler, he herded the *remuda*, watched over the wagon teams and helped to set up or tear down the camp. When the time came he even sunk fence poles and rode the wire. And when his job was done, and old Coronado's *despoblado* was fenced and criss-crossed with rails and highways, he faded away like the buffalo and the Indian before him.

The last years saw the end of the free range, the coming of bigger and bigger ranches, the associations and cattle companies. Cowboys still ride today. Cattle are rounded-up, roped and branded using all the inherited Spanish–Mexican skills you have been reading about. But modern life has caught up with the cowboy, and estate wagons are parked in front of the hitching rail while helicopters land by the corral. All in little more than one man's lifetime!

H. L. Davis, who writes fine western stories, sums it up when he talks of 'Old Man Isbell'.

'He lived his eighty-five years through the most splendidly coloured history that one man could ever have lived through in the world – the Civil War, the Indian campaigns in the West, the mining days, the cattle-kings, the long-line freighters, the road agents, the stockmen's wars – the changing, with a swiftness and decision unknown to history before, of a country and its people; yes, and of a nation. Not as a spectator, either. He lived in the middle of every bit of it, and had a hand in every phase.'*

* *Out West* Vol 1, Jack Schaefer (ed.), London; André Deutsch, 1959.

If you want to read more about cowboys and the Old West here is a short list of good books on the subject. Of course, as you learn more you will have to turn to the real histories and stories for information. Look for the last four titles in the adult section of your library.

Men of the Old West by Robert J. Hoare (Chatto, 1972): *Wagons Over the Mountains* by Edith McCall (Odhams, n.d.): *Sioux Arrow* by John Robb (Hutchinson, n.d.): *The Discovery of the American West* by Charles Chilton (Hamlyn, 1969): *The Penguin Book of the American West* by David Lavender (Penguin, 1969): *Out West,* a fine selection of stories, selected by Jack Schaefer the author of *Shane*, which will introduce you to many exciting western writers (Andre Deutsch, 1959).

And if you really want to try one of the best books of western adventure ever written see if you can find a copy of Francis Parkman's *The Oregon Trail* (Holt, Rinehart & Winston, 1849).